RECORDING
ƒINANCIAL INFORMATION

GAIL SHARRATT

Hodder & Stoughton

I dedicate this book to my family –
especially my Mum – who supported me
throughout this project.

The publishers would like to thank Life File
for permission to reproduce Figures 1.5 and
2.1.

A catalogue record for this title is available from The British Library

ISBN 0 340 655224

First published 1997
Impression number   10 9 8 7 6 5 4 3 2 1
Year   2002 2001 2000 1999 1998 1997

Copyright © 1997 Gail Sharratt

All rights reserved. No part of this publication may be reproduced or transmitted in any form or by any means, electronic or mechanical, including photocopy, recording, or any information storage and retrieval system, without permission in writing from the publisher or under licence from the Copyright Licensing Agency Limited. Further details of such licences (for reprographic reproduction) may be obtained from the Copyright Licensing Agency Limited, of 90 Tottenham Court Road, London W1P 9HE.

Typeset by Fakenham Photosetting Limited, Fakenham, Norfolk

Printed in Great Britain for Hodder & Stoughton Educational, a division of Hodder Headline Plc, 338 Euston Road, London NW1 3BH by Scotprint, Musselburgh, Scotland.

Contents

Introduction	1
Introduction to GNVQs' course content and structure	3
1 Recording and calculating simple financial transactions	6
2 Calculating and recording pay	17
3 Recording and monitoring stock movements	35
4 Monitoring transactions against a given budget	43
Multiple-choice questions	50
Glossary	54
References	57
Answers to multiple-choice questions	58
Index	59

Introduction

I wrote this book for both teachers and students on the Intermediate General National Vocational Qualification (GNVQ) in Business, who are completing optional unit six – Recording Financial Information.

The book fulfils two main roles. Firstly, it provides a source of information for students who are gathering evidence for their portfolios. Secondly, it contains tasks, activities, resources and assignments for teachers of the subject, who have – in the past – found it hard to gather information for the unit.

It also covers a variety of key skills which are identified as and when they occur.

Note: To complete the chapter on calculating pay, it is necessary to refer to the published tax and National Insurance tables, as issued by HMSO.

Introduction to GNVQs' course content and structure

Both NVQs and GNVQs can be awarded at various levels – most commonly Foundation, Intermediate and Advanced. This book is primarily for use on the Intermediate course which means that on completion the student will have a qualification equivalent to four GCSEs.

To successfully complete a GNVQ at any level you must gather evidence which is presented in the form of a portfolio. Evidence can come in many forms. It can be handwritten letters or reports, computerised accounts, video tapes of presentations, tape recordings of discussions or even displays and graphics. This means that even if you find it difficult to put your thoughts down on paper, there are many other ways for you to gain the evidence you need for your portfolio.

On the Intermediate GNVQ, you have to gather evidence to cover a specific number of units. Four of these units are mandatory, i.e. you have to take these in order to gain the award. Three of these units are accompanied by end tests – multiple-choice exams which test your knowledge and understanding of the subject. These can be taken three times during the length of the course – and also re-sat if they are not passed during that time.

You also have to complete two other units. These vary from establishment to establishment depending on the knowledge base of the teachers concerned. Some of the options available are consumer protection, personal finance, business enterprise and even foreign languages. These units do not have an end test.

Along with your four mandatory and two optional or additional units, you must also complete what are termed 'key skills' in Application of Number, Communication and Information Technology. These are transferable skills and are the same for all Intermediate courses. However, they are delivered (or taught) in a vocational context. Therefore, the evidence a person gathers for a key skill on the Business GNVQ may be different than that of a GNVQ Engineering student – even though it is for the same skill.

What makes up a unit?

All units (whether mandatory, optional, additional or key skill) are divided up into several layers – each getting more specific. The first of these is called an element. Units can be made up of two, three or four elements. For example, in *Recording Financial Information* there are four elements 6.1, 6.2, 6.3 and 6.4. Each element covers a different aspect of recording financial information. Element 6.1, for instance, covers recording and calculating simple financial transactions, while element 6.2 covers calculating pay. This breaks a subject down into smaller, more manageable parts.

Next, we can break down each element into 'performance criteria' (or PCs). There can be anything from three to seven PCs in an element. A PC states what a student must be able to do – for example calculate pay, discuss issues or design promotional material.

A further subdivision of PCs is the 'range statement'. This breaks down the PC into precise areas of skill, knowledge and understanding in which the student must meet the PCs. There are varying numbers of range statements accompanying PCs.

Unfortunately, there is more to it than that. When you put together your portfolio of evidence, you have to meet certain requirements. This is to make sure that everyone's intermediate qualification is of an equal level. To ensure this, you have to meet what are known as evidence indicators. These identify the **minimum** evidence that a student's portfolio must contain, in order to gain the award.

But all is not lost! Along with all of this does come help in two forms – one is amplification. This clarifies key terms used in the element, sometimes with examples to help interpret and illustrate the key terms, and provides details on the depth and scope of expected coverage. Lastly – you will be pleased to know – there is extra guidance (for teachers and lecturers) on how to deliver the unit. This also indicates if it is possible to link work between elements.

1

Recording and calculating simple financial transactions

Recording and calculating simple financial transactions

Recording financial transactions

Why do businesses go to the trouble of recording the financial transactions completed within their organisations? Some reasons are explored below.

INFORM MANAGERS AND OWNERS

Although it is sometimes true that the owner of a business is also the manager of it, it is not always the case. To make everyday decisions, or those of more importance, both managers and owners must have the correct information on which to base those decisions. A lot of the time, that information is financial – whether it is how much money is in the bank, what the company has purchased in the previous week or what discounts they receive from their suppliers. The more accurate and up to date the information at hand is, the better the decisions which can be made thereby benefiting the organisation.

FULFIL STATUTORY REQUIREMENTS

There are some financial documents that an organisation has to fill in by law. These are:

- VAT returns
- Payslips
- Income tax returns
- National Insurance contributions.

In some cases, this is because the information is required by the government to keep its financial house in order, in others, it is to fulfil obligations to employees. In either case, failure to provide the correct documentation can lead to prosecution.

FIGURE 1.1 *A business needs up-to-date, accurate information*

> **Key terms**
>
> VAT (Value Added Tax) – A percentage added to the price of goods sold by businesses, which is collected by HM Customs and Excise.

MONITOR PERFORMANCE

Setting targets and monitoring whether they have been achieved or not is one way that an organisation can grow, spot problems within itself and solve those problems. For example, if an organisation finds that it is running short of money in its bank account, it may look to its financial records to see exactly where the money is going. When it finds out where the problem is, it can then hopefully take measures to alleviate it.

Recording transactions

ACCOUNTING RECORDS

To make sure that they can accomplish all of the above, businesses keep a standard set of accounting records. These are described, with examples, on the following pages.

Cash book

An organisation's income and expenditure is recorded in its cash book – income being the money received by an organisation, and expenditure being money which is paid out by the organisation. In financial documents income is recorded on the left-hand side while expenditure can be found on the right.

As can be seen from Figure 1.2, a large amount of information can be stored in the cash book in a limited amount of space. This makes it a useful way of obtaining information at a glance – where the company has gained money (income) and where it has been spent (payments), in the past few days or weeks. For instance, the company may ring and enquire whether a payment they made yesterday by post has reached its destination yet. They would be able to quote the cheque number and its details.

Purchase day book

This book is used when recording the purchases made by an organisation. Of course the business has to pay for the purchases it makes, and it will get this information in the form of an invoice from its supplier. As soon as an invoice is received, it should be entered into the purchase day book, so that accurate records are kept at all times. Of course, organisations are free to lay out their purchase day book as they see fit, but there is a standard set of information across the board that most businesses will want to keep in there. These are:

- The date the invoice arrived
- The name of the supplier
- The number on the supplier's invoice
- The price (excluding VAT)
- VAT
- The total on the invoice.

They may also want to have a progress column, which would show the status of the

Recording and calculating simple financial transactions

Receipts

	Income				Sales			
Date	Item	Bank	Ref.	VAT	Stationary	Cards	Sweets	House
3 May	Till	940	1	140	800			
	Till	205.62	2	30.62		175		
	Till	258.5	3	38.5			220	
	Till	329	4	49				280
3 May	Total	1733.12		258.12	800	175	220	280

- details of where money came from
- details of what was sold
- details of money coming into the business

Payments

	Expenditure					Stock			
Date	Item	Cheque no.	Ref.	Bank	VAT	Stat	Sundries	Wages	Rent
3 May	ABC Ltd	3459	2	352.5	52.5		300		
3 May	Allsorts Sweets	3460	3	235	35		200		
3 May	Staff	3461		175				175	
3 May	Landlord	3462		200					200
3 May	Total			962.5	87.5		500	175	200

- details of where money is going to
- details of what money was spent on
- details of money leaving the business

FIGURE 1.2 *An example of a cash book*

payment. This column would be updated every time an invoice is paid or queried.

Of course, some companies may want to have further information in their purchase day book. This could include:

- The address of the supplier
- The telephone number of the above
- A contact name at the organisation in case of queries
- The initials of the person who entered the details into the day book.

> ### Key terms
>
> Supplier – A person or organisation from whom goods are bought.

Sales day book

In any company, it is vital to keep a record of how much money it is owed. This is basic common sense! This information is recorded in the sales day book (see Figure 1.4). When a customer purchases goods from an organisation, they will be sent an invoice and, for every invoice which is sent out, there should be a corresponding entry in the sales day book. The company will also keep a copy of every invoice which is sent out, for its future reference, in case of any queries which may arise.

So, just what information is stored in a sales day book? Well, again, this may differ slightly from company to company in its layout and in certain details, but the basic facts remain fairly consistent. These are:

- Date of invoice
- A description of the item (this could be abbreviated or coded) or the customer's name
- The invoice number. This will be unique to the firm and to the invoice. It is used for filing and for identifying a particular invoice in the case of queries
- The price without VAT (this is known as the net amount)
- VAT: calculated for most products at 17.5 per cent
- Invoice amount: the total amount the customer pays (in other words the net amount plus VAT)

Date	Supplier	Invoice number	Price excluding VAT	VAT	Invoice total	Progress
6.5	R Patel Ltd	0084C	£270.00	£47.25	£317.25	Sent cheque
7.5	Crewe Alexandra F.C.	3712	£140.00	£24.50	£164.50	
7.5	Harris City Technology College	XV17	£450.00	£78.75	£528.75	

FIGURE 1.3 *An example of a purchase day book*

Recording and calculating simple financial transactions

✎ Discounts: it is common practice in business to offer discounts for various reasons, either for bulk purchases or for prompt payment. If this is the case, the appropriate discount will also be shown.

> **Key terms**
>
> Discount – A percentage or amount deducted from the total amount outstanding on a purchase, usually for bulk buying or for prompt payment.

Returns day book

Some times, goods which have been ordered by an organisation are returned to the company from which they were ordered. This could happen because the goods were found to be damaged on delivery, or because the wrong goods have been sent, or too many were delivered (see Figure 1.5). Whatever the reason, the company needs to make a note that these goods have been returned. This takes place in the returns day book.

As can be seen from Figure 1.6, there are various pieces of information which need to be recorded in the returns day book. Obviously, not all returns day book will be identical, but this one will give you an idea as to what can be recorded and will include:

Date	Customer item	Price excl. VAT	Invoice number	Invoice amount	VAT	Discount	Progress
3-May	Alan Burrows – hairdressers	£300.00	379	£352.50	£52.50		Paid
4-May	Crewe and Nantwich Borough Council	£650.00	380	£763.75	£113.75		Phoned again 20/5
20-May	Joseph Heler Ltd	£220.00	381	£258.50	£38.50		Paid

FIGURE 1.4 *An example of a sales day book*

FIGURE 1.5 *Deliveries should be checked on arrival*

- Date of returned goods
- Company to which the goods have been returned
- Invoice no. goods originally ordered on
- Description of goods returned
- Value of goods returned
- Reason for the return
- Progress column – to record any action which has been taken to follow up the reason for the return.

Orders

When a company wants to buy something from another company, it places an order (see Figure 1.7). This is done on an order form which, in many cases, is unique to the company placing the order, as it may have the company logo and name and address printed at the top of the form. Apart from that, it also contains the following information which will be needed by the company filling the order:

- The name and address of the supplier
- The address the goods are to be delivered to
- The name or signature of the person who has authorised the order
- The date the order was placed
- The date the goods are to be delivered by
- The order number (unique to that particular order)
- The quantity of each item required
- A description (which may include a code or abbreviation) of the item required
- The price for each unit of the goods required
- The total amount for each item required (the quantity multiplied by the price).

Invoices

An invoice is sent to a business as an official request for payment for goods or services supplied by another organisation. It shows the details of the transactions which have taken place, such as the details of the purchase, the amount and the order number (see Figure 1.8).

- What are the current rates of VAT?
- Are there any items on which we **do not** pay VAT? What are they?

Date	Customer item	Invoice number	Description of goods returned	Reason for return	Progress
24-May	Langley Computers	367	Computer desk – pine	Scratched surface	Replacement delivered – 29 May
26-May	Wrights Builders	376	Filing cabinet – 4-drawer	Faulty lock	Investigating
1-June	Cummings Chauffeurs	380	Key rack	Wrong colour delivered	Replacement sent

FIGURE 1.6 *An example of a returns day book*

Recording and calculating simple financial transactions

Harris City Technology College
Maberley Road
Upper Norwood
London SE19 2JH
Tel: 0181 771 2261   Fax: 0181 771 3382

Order form

To:	Name & delivery address

Authorised	Date of order	Date required	Order number

Quantity	Please supply the following items	Unit price	Amount

The order number must appear on all invoices and delivery notes.
Signed and agreed:

FIGURE 1.7 *An example of an order form*

Harris City Technology College
Maberley Road
Upper Norwood
London SE19 2JH

Tel: 0181 771 2261   Fax: 0181 771 3382

Invoice

Customer:	Delivery address

Your order number	Date sent	Invoice date	Invoice number

Quantity	Description	Unit price	Amount

Sub total
VAT (17.5%)
Total

FIGURE 1.8 *An example of an invoice*

RECORDING INFORMATION

When it comes to recording financial information, there are obvious advantages and disadvantages to keeping that information on a computer as opposed to on paper and in books. Despite the disadvantages (which we will discuss in a moment) more and more companies are starting to transfer their record-keeping onto computers. Some of the advantages are listed below:

- ☺ Data can be retrieved quickly and easily
- ☺ Data can be changed without having to re-type the whole document
- ☺ Storage space is condensed (many documents which would take up a whole filing cabinet can now be stored on just a few floppy disks)
- ☺ Today's school leavers are now more computer-literate than ever before
- ☺ There is a wide range of computer software available to fulfil the needs of most businesses
- ☺ The price of computer hardware is decreasing all the time
- ☺ If the correct software for your company is not available, you can commission a program especially designed to fit your needs.

Of course, as mentioned before, there are disadvantages to using IT in businesses:

- ☹ Many people's jobs have been taken over by automation or by IT in offices. These people have been made redundant
- ☹ The cost of IT (while reducing all the time) can still be expensive, especially for small businesses
- ☹ Staff (especially those who have little or no experience using computers) will need to be re-trained
- ☹ Computers and IT become out of date so rapidly that a company which invests thousands of pounds in computer hardware and software may find that it has become obsolete within 10 years and needs to be replaced
- ☹ If the computer is damaged or the disks destroyed, then the business will be in trouble as they may have no record of the transactions they have made for a considerable period of time (this is where having a backup system comes into play).

assignment

★ **EVIDENCE INDICATOR**

An explanation of the purposes of accounting records for financial transactions.

★ **KEY SKILLS CONTRIBUTED TOWARDS**

IT
Communication

★ **SCENARIO**

You work for a medium-sized organisation which has recently taken on several new employees of school-leaving age. Your manager has been asked to put together an induction pack for the new employees, and has asked you to write the section detailing the work involved in the accounts department.

★ **TASKS**

1 Produce a front cover for your section of the induction pack. This should be produced using IT and should incorporate combined text and graphics from two packages.

2 The main body of the text should explain the following purposes of accounting information:

- To inform managers and owners
- To fulfil statutory obligations
- To monitor performance.

All information should be accurate and relevant to the booklet. The text should be legible and the meaning clear. It should be spell-checked and contain proper punctuation and grammar.

3 The main body of the text should also include images at appropriate times so as to enhance the meaning of the text.

★ **DEADLINE**

assignment

★ **EVIDENCE INDICATOR**

Notes and calculations of simple financial transactions which include an explanation of accounting records.

★ **KEY SKILLS**

IT
Communication

★ **TASKS**

1 Prepare – in draft form – a report which explains the purpose of accounting records for financial transactions.

2 Using an appropriate IT package, prepare a neat copy of the work and print out a hard copy.

3 Import suitable graphics to illustrate the points made. Make another hard copy.

4 *In a separate report, give an explanation of how you worked safely on the computer, in line with good working practices.*

★ **DEADLINE**

2

Calculating and recording pay

Calculating pay

ATTENDANCE RECORDS

There are several ways for an organisation to monitor and record how long its employees work for in a given time period, (normally per day over the period of a week).

In manual or blue-collar employment, much use is made of clock cards. Employees are required to clock in and clock out using an individual card which they keep for a week. Normally, the clock is placed in a conspicuous position so that it is difficult for people to forget to clock in or out. The time on a clock card is measured using the standard 24-hour clock; however, in some organisations use is made of the 100-minute hour. This records the minutes in hours by dividing the hour into 100 equal parts rather than 60. The advantage of this is that it is easier to find the sum of the hours worked, as you do not have to think in terms of base 60. To find the equivalent in a 100-minute hour as opposed to a 60-minute hour, multiply the number of minutes by 1.66 (approximately). An advantage of clocking in and out is that it is difficult for people to falsify their work hours, as the clock is virtually tamper-proof. You could of course get someone to clock in and out for you, but, as clock cards are often used as an attendance check in case of fire, this is a dangerous course of action.

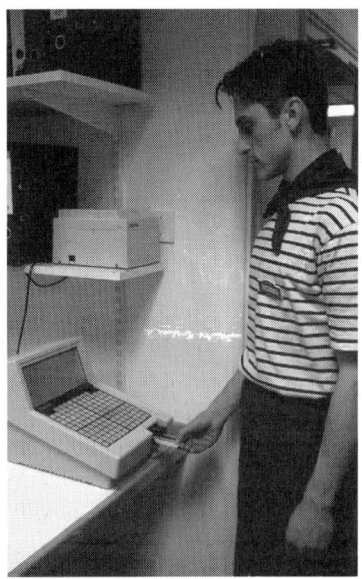

FIGURE 2.1 *Clocking in at work on an electronic machine*

Calculate the following clocking in and out times in the 24-hour clock, using both the 60-minute hour and the 100-minute hour.

Clock in	Clock out	Clock in	Clock out
7.45 am	10.00 am	11.15 am	3.30 pm
9.15 am	12.30 pm	1.05 pm	5.55 pm

Example:

When you clock in after lunch on a 24-hour clock at 1.15 pm, the clock card will record 13.15 as your clock-in time. However, in a 100-minute hour, this will be recorded at 13.25 as it is quarter past the hour. Likewise, 1.30 pm would be either 13.30 on the 24-hour clock or 13.50 using the 100-minute hour.

Another method of recording attendance is via signing in and out. This is found mostly in clerical or white-collar work such as in offices. There will usually be a set of

Calculating and recording pay

FIGURE 2.2 *An example of a timesheet*

timesheets located at a convenient point around the office or workplace. Each employee will have their own sheet within this set. It is up to the individual employee to mark in each working day at what time they start work, at what time they break for lunch, start work after lunch and finish work to go home. Obviously, this system has its advantages and disadvantages over the clock card system. However, you are relying very much more on the honesty of individual workers to fill in their timesheet accurately.

NATIONAL INSURANCE AND TAX TABLES

National insurance – what is it?

Just before their sixteenth birthday, every UK citizen receives their National Insurance number. This is sent to them by the government, and is a way to enable every adult in the UK to be identified when it comes to work records, tax records and even criminal records. Everybody who works and earns more than a specified amount each week pays national insurance (or NI). This is paid to the government and is used to pay for your pension, unemployment or other benefits (such as sick pay), and for the National Health Service. **At the same time, your employer also pays towards your national insurance so that for every pound you pay, they pay a corresponding – but higher – amount as well**. If you lose your job, the amount of NI you have paid while you were working and the amount of time you have been employed are taken into account to assess the amount of unemployment benefit you are entitled to – if any. Your NI contributions (commonly known as your stamp) also dictate the amount of state pension you receive when you reach the age of 65. Years ago, women were treated unequally where NI contributions were concerned: as it was commonly assumed that their husbands would provide for them in their old age, thousands of married women were advised not to pay the full NI contribution which would have got them a full pension. When it became apparent that these women were outliving their husbands – sometimes by two decades – the advice was changed and now everybody is advised to pay their full stamp.

Income tax – what is it and why pay it?

Income tax is paid by most people who are employed in paid work. It is paid to the government and is one of their main sources of revenue. Over the years the basic rate of income tax has changed, depending on the political party in power and the economic situation of the time. Overall, Labour has had higher income tax levels than the Conservatives; this is because, in the past, Labour spent more money on public services such as education, transport and housing, and so needed the extra money to finance this.

So, that is what NI and tax is. But knowing how much of each an employee and employer has to pay is a tricky business. As lots of small businesses do not have an employee who only calculates pay, the government have tried to make it as simple as possible for businesses to calculate the contributions which have to be paid. They produce a set of tables each financial year which provide businesses with a 'ready reckoner' as to exactly how much tax and National Insurance must be paid.

Recording pay

PAYROLL

An organisation's payroll is simply a list of the people it employs. This can be kept manually – as in Figure 2.3. As you can see, this example shows the employees' names and their normal working hours.

Another method of recording a company's payroll is on a computer using a database. Keeping the payroll on the computer has a number of advantages to keeping it on paper. Firstly, more information can be stored about an individual in one place – i.e. name, address, number of years' service, NI number. This may be stored on a screen like the one shown in Figure 2.4.

PAGE 3 of 4

WEEKLY STAFF RECORD
PL101B

WEEK ENDING 10.2.96.

NAME	MON		TUES		WED		THURS		FRI		SAT		SUN	
	IN	OUT	IN	OUT	IN	OUT	IN	OUT	IN	OUT	IN	OUT	IN	OUT
D BROADHURST	700	PR	700		600		700		700		500			
A BOTHAM	800	MR	800		800		800		800		800			
B COLLINS	HOL	PR	600		600		500		600		5.30			
L CUNLIFFE	700	CR	700		700		700		700		800			
P DYKES	4.30	BR	4.30		4.30		4.30		4.30		4.30			
J GLOVER	700	CR	600		800		800		800		HOL			
N GEE	OFF	CS	600		6.10		6.30		600		700			
D GRIFFITHS	600	PR	600		600		500		600		500			
T GRUNNER	HOL	PR	HOL		700		700		600		700			
T JUMP	600	CS	600		600		600		600		700			
M LEAR	5.30	PA	5.30		5.30		4.30		5.30		4.30			
A McMEEKIN	HOL	CS	6.45		6.45		6.45		6.45		6.30			
P MYERS	800	CR	800		800		7.15		800		700			
T MYERS	600	PA	600		600		500		600		500			
G OTTER	600	PA	600		600		500		600		500			
A PERRY	600	CR	600		600		600		600		600			
A SHONE	700	CR	700		700		10.00		700		700			
J WASHINGTON	700	CR	700		700		700		HOL		700			
M WILKINS	600	PR	700		700		500		700		700			
J WOODCOCK	600	PR	600		600		HOL		HOL		HOL			
S WASHINGTON	700	MR			700		800		800		800			
K FOWLES	SICK													

FIGURE 2.3 *An example of a payroll*

Recording financial information

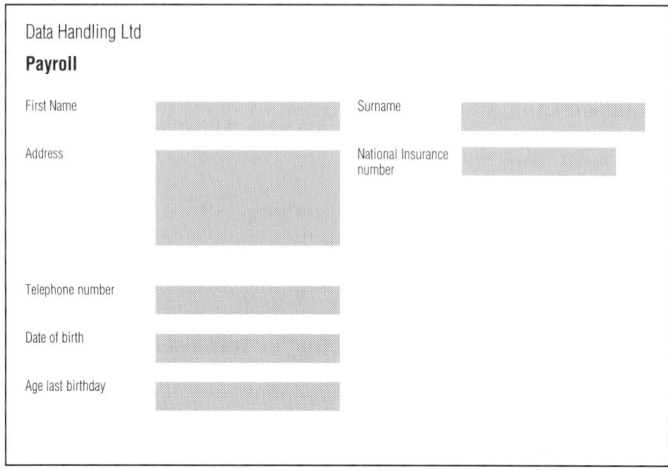

FIGURE 2.4 *An example of a computer-stored payroll*

PAYSLIPS

It does not matter how you get paid, whether it is weekly, monthly, by the hour or by commission, whether you get your money paid directly to you, or paid into the bank or whether you are a manager or a shop worker – you will receive some form of payslip.

Payslips come in all shapes and sizes, but must show – by law – several pieces of information. These are:

- Your gross pay
- Your income tax deducted or refunded
- Your national insurance contributions
- Your net pay.

FIGURE 2.5 *All payslips must show the same basic information*

Alongside these, there are several other things that you may see on your payslip. Depending on your individual circumstances these may be pension contributions to a company pension scheme, repayments to your employer if you have taken out a loan with them for computer equipment or a year's rail travel pass. It may be that you have maintenance for a child deducted from your wages or that you have a county court judgement against you; it could also be in the form of union subscriptions, tea money or for discounted purchases from your employer. All of these items and more can be deducted from your pay before you receive it. These are called deductions *at source*. Lots of people find it easier to pay for things like a pension or travel this way, as it saves them the hassle of having to put money aside on a regular basis – not everyone is good at saving!

Below is an example of a blank payslip. The details will be added and then it will be printed off using a computer.

Note: When you start work it is important for you to keep your payslips safe, as you may need to produce them for inspection by your local tax office.

STANDARD NATIONAL FORMS

Organisations all over the country have to abide by the same practices when it comes to informing their employees and the government about the national insurance and tax they have paid – it would be very confusing if everybody used different forms and sent in different information. Some people would, of course, send in the correct details, but others – through no fault of their own – would find it impossible to grasp what the government was looking for. Therefore, the government produces sets of forms – standard national forms (SNF) – which all have varying purposes and which can be filled in by businesses from all over the country. The most heard of SNF is the P45. This is often associated with losing your job but is, in fact, a statement of who your last employer was, what your tax code is and how much tax you paid in the tax year to date (if applicable). When you start a new

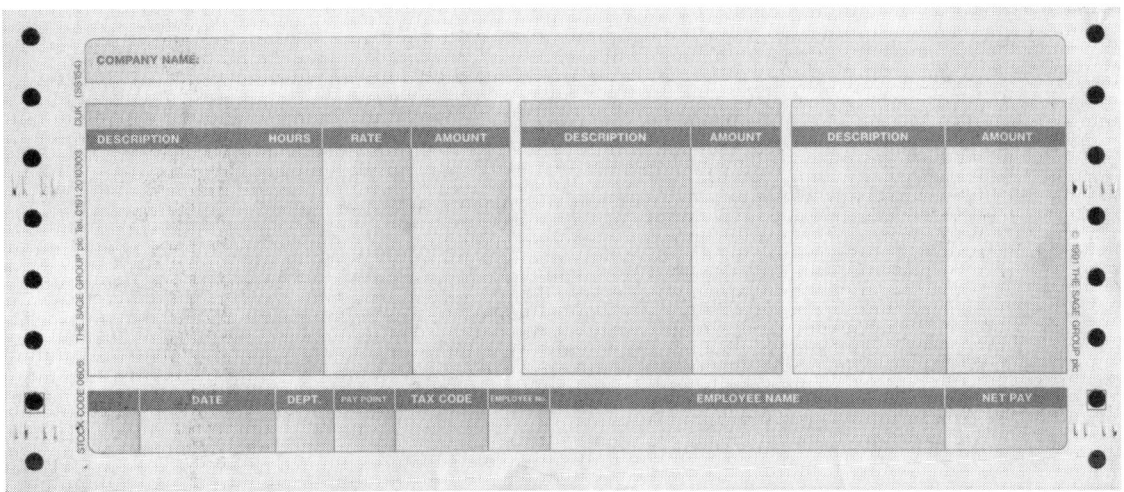

FIGURE 2.6 *An example of a blank payslip*

job you give your P45 to your new employer and they then know how much tax to deduct (if any) from your wages. If you do not know your tax code or do not have a P45, you will be put on what is known as emergency tax. This will most likely be more than you should be paying at the time and you may have to apply for a rebate in the future – an inconvenience we could all avoid.

WAGES AND SALARIES

What is the difference between a wage and a salary? You cannot measure the difference in terms of the amount of money they represent, as someone who earns a wage can earn more or less than someone who is paid a salary (or vice versa). You can start to look at the difference in terms of the types of occupations which earn either a wage or a salary. It is assumed that manual, blue-collar or unskilled or semi-skilled occupations are more likely to earn a wage, while white-collar, skilled or office-based jobs are more likely to earn a salary – but that is not always the case either. The basic difference is that when you earn a wage, it can vary each week (or month), as it is dependent upon the number of hours you work, or the number of goods you produce or sell, i.e. it is variable. However, a salary is more of a fixed income, which would vary due to unusual circumstances, such as absence or sick leave, but does not depend on the number of hours you work.

Time rates

If you are paid a wage (see above) it is likely to be dependent on the amount of time you have worked for. This is measured as we saw earlier on clock cards or on signing in sheets.

Bonus rates

Not everybody works for a set amount per hour or per week. For some people, bonuses are also part of their wages – if not every week, then at certain times of the year. The most famous of these is the Christmas bonus, which is a thank you from an employer for the hard work an employee has done throughout the year.

However, there are other types of bonuses. Another common way of adding a bonus to your wage packet is through performance-related pay (PRP). This is calculated by checking your performance against a list of pre-set criteria, and your bonus is paid accordingly. These criteria are often very subjective i.e. they can be hard to define, or it can be difficult to tell whether you have met them or not. Some examples of bonus criteria at a real organisation, Harris City Technology College, are:

⑦ Have you performed your job as described in your job description?

⑦ Have you organised any extra-curricular activities?

activity

Look at the job advertisements below and calculate the average wage per week for each. Which gives the best reward?

Jobs – Wages

EXPERIENCED SALES ASSISTANT REQUIRED

★ 35 hours per week
★ £3.99 per hour
★ 15% discount on purchases

Lynne's Lockets

Stylist

40 hours per week
£4.10 per hour
Free hair care

Apply in writing to

Helen's Hair Emporium

Nanny REQUIRED

✻

25 hours per week
£3.50 per hour

✻

Apply in writing to

Nina's Nursery

PART-TIME Carpenter

required

15 hours per week
£5.30 per hour

Apply in writing to

Bill's Builders

Jobs – Salaries

SALES MANAGER/ESS

£14,500 p.a.
Clothes allowance – 10% of salary
Company car

DAVE'S DOORBELLS

PART-TIME SOLICITOR

20 out of 35 hours worked each week
£20,000 pro rata
Bonus scheme
Luncheon Vouchers (15 per week)

Bev's Barristers

FULLY-QUALIFIED ACCOUNTANT

£16,000 p.a.
Medical Insurance
Pension Scheme

PRYOR & SEIVRIGHT ACCOUNTANTS

Children's Party Organiser

£15,000 p.a.
Company car
Free cowboy outfit

Paul's Party Planners

- Have you performed any duties on a regular basis over and above those described in your job description?
- What standard has the work you have undertaken been carried out at?

There is one major problem with bonus systems: they are often subject to what psychologists term the 'halo effect'. This occurs when a person's bonus is being calculated. If the person responsible for recommending the amount of a person's bonus likes the said individual, then there is more chance of them awarding a higher mark – even if the person has carried out their work to the same standard as a second employee, whom the person awarding the bonus either does not know well or dislikes. This can create problems in PRP, which is often meant to be used as a motivating factor!

There are even more types of bonuses. People employed in the construction business often get a bonus if they complete a project before the scheduled date. This can also occur in the computer software business. Another example is sales people who, as well as commission on their sales, may be paid a bonus if they sell over a specific target set for the week or month.

Bonuses do not always have to be paid in cash, they can also be paid in kind in the form of cars, holidays, gift vouchers and other incentives – although these would not necessarily appear on a person's payslip.

Commission

Sales people are most well known for being paid by commission. Commission is a percentage of a sale which is earned by the sales person for making the sale. Some sales people are paid on a commission-only basis, which means that the amount they get paid is directly related to the amount they sell. Other sales people get a basic wage plus commission. The percentage of commission paid also varies from employer to employer. Some sale positions which pay commission include the following areas:

- Double glazing
- Holidays
- Cars
- Cosmetics
- Computers
- Insurance
- Door to door
- Electrical equipment
- Encyclopedias.

Overtime

Most employees who are paid a wage will know how many hours they are expected to work in order to earn their wage. If they work additional hours, they may be eligible for overtime: this is extra pay for working hours over and above those for which you are contracted. This is paid at a higher rate of pay than normal. It could be one-and-a-half, two, two-and-a-half or more times the normal rate. This depends on the organisation, the position held, the day, number of hours and time of year involved!

Piece rates

In some occupations, your wage does not depend on the amount of time you spend at work, but on how productively you use the time there. For instance, it could be possible for an employee to clock on to work and then pretend to work for the day, when in reality they have not contributed to the work carried out that day. As long as they do not get caught by their employers, they will still get paid. A way around this for employers who may have a high turnover of staff, or whose employees repeatedly carry out the same task (such as in the garment industry), is to pay employees depending on how many of an item they produce. This way, the more work that is carried out, the higher the employee's wages. This stops the temptation to be lazy and – in theory – is a way to motivate employees.

Annual rates

Unlike the advertisements shown previously (see page 25) for jobs with hourly rates, if an occupation draws a salary it is not expressed monthly (which is how often salaries are paid) but is expressed as an annual rate. You will see that after the figures given will be the initials p.a. which stand for *per annum* (Latin for *every year*). Some of the vacancies on page 25 are also part-time, but they may still have a full-time salary attached. If this is the case, the term *pro rata* will be added next to the salary. This means that you may not receive the full amount stated, but it is apportioned over the amount of time you do work. For example: if the position states that the salary is £15,000 p.a. pro rata for three days a week, a quick way to estimate the real salary you would earn would be to divide the salary by five (number of days in a working week) and then times that by three (the number of days you would be working). This would estimate that instead of the £15,000 advertised, you would receive about £9,000 p.a. *before* deductions. Some of the salaries you see for jobs will seem high, however this is gross pay – you still have to pay tax and national insurance on these salaries, which comes to approximately a third or more of the salary – so the salary may not be as high as it seems.

In the following worked example we will be

> ### Key terms
>
> Gross pay – The amount of pay before any deductions.
> Net pay – The amount of pay you actually receive – after deductions for tax, NI etc.

looking at how to record the pay earned by a manual worker, paid using the manual calculation method.

The person we will be looking at is Jonathan Burrows, a farm worker at a cheese factory. He clocks on and off using a clock card, a copy of which is shown on page 28.

Recording financial information

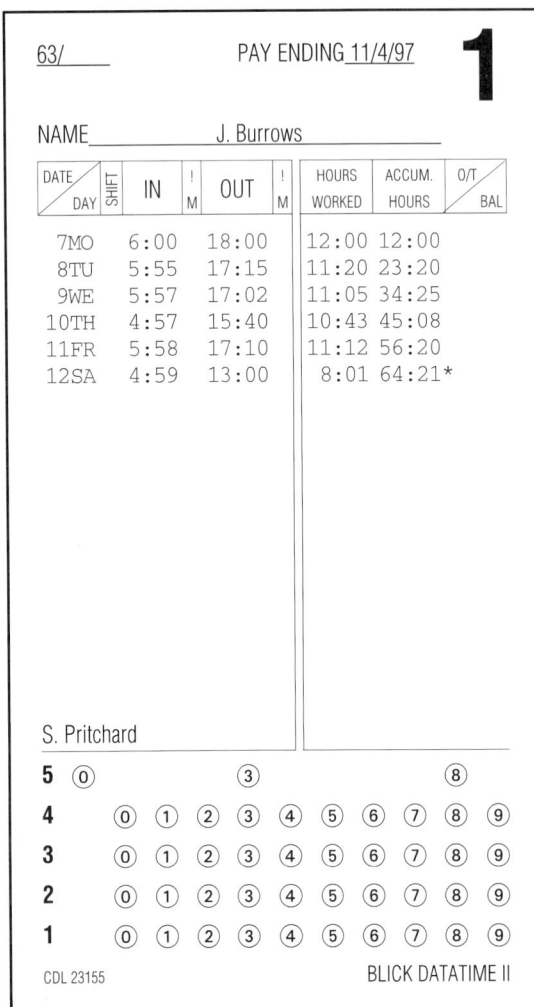

FIGURE 2.7 *An example of a clock card*

Jonathan's work details are as follows:

- Basic hours = 39
- Tax code = 273L
- Pay – normal = £4.62
- Pay – overtime = £6.93

Jonathan is supposed to clock on at the following times each day:

- Monday   – 6.00 am
- Tuesday – 6.00 am
- Wednesday – 6.00 am
- Thursday – 5.00 am
- Friday   – 6.00 am
- Saturday – 5.00 am.

The first stage in calculating Jonathan's wage is to work out the amount of hours he worked during the week by examining the clock card (see Figure 2.7).

As you can see from his clock card, Jonathan has clocked on a couple of minutes early on five out of the six days. He will not be paid for these minutes, and so they must be deducted from the amount of hours worked.

Look at the * symbol on the clock card. This figure is the total hours worked for the week (in this case 64 hours and 21 minutes). However, he clocked on a total of 14 minutes early throughout the week, which have to be deducted from this – making a total of 64 hours and seven minutes.

As Jonathan works all over the farm, it is unreasonable for us to expect him to clock off at lunch time. Therefore, we have to deduct time for his lunch. He is allowed 45 minutes per day – apart from Saturday when he finished at lunch time anyway. Therefore there is a further three hours 45 minutes to deduct from this total leaving 60 hours and 22 minutes for which he is actually paid. Quite a difference from the 64.21 recorded at first glance on the clock card!

Jonathan is supposed to work a minimum of 39 hours per week. Anything over and above that is classed as overtime. This leaves us with two different rates of pay – basic @ £4.62 per hour and overtime rate @ £6.93 per hour. Therefore we can calculate that Jonathan should receive (rounded up or down to the nearest quarter hour):

Calculating and recording pay

39 hours @ £4.62 = £180.18
21¼ hours @ £6.93 = £147.26
60¼ hours = £327.44

So, we can see that Jonathan's **gross** pay (without any deductions) is £327.44 for that week. However, now comes the tricky part – working out how much tax and NI Jonathan pays for the week! For this we need to refer to the tax tables which are published by the government. Tax table A can be obtained from your local tax office, or the finance department of your school or college.

We also need a new form to record all the information. A copy of this can be gained from your local tax office, but the basic layout is as follows:

Employee's name:					Tax code:				Year:		
Week no.	Pay on which NI to be paid	Employee's NI	Employer's NI	Total NI	Week no.	Pay in the week/ month	Total pay to date	Total free pay to date	Total taxable pay to date	Total tax due to date	Tax deducted or refunded
1					1						
2					2						
3					3						
4					4						
5					5						
6					6						
7					7						
8					8						
9					9						
10					10						

TABLE 1 *Blank tax form*

On this form we need to input the first pieces of information we have gathered so far:

Employee's name:					Tax code:				Year:		
Week no.	Pay on which NI to be paid	Employee's NI	Employer's NI	Total NI	Week no.	Pay in the week/ month	Total pay to date	Total free pay to date	Total taxable pay to date	Total tax due to date	Tax deducted or refunded
1					1	327.44	327.44	52.68			
2					2						
3					3						
4					4						
5					5						
6					6						
7					7						
8					8						
9					9						
10					10						

TABLE 2 *Pay to date*

Now we can start to calculate the deductions. To do this we need to look at the first set of tax tables – known as 'pay adjustment tables' (or Table A). Table A consists of 52 pages – one for each week of the year. It allows you to calculate how much money you can earn – for any one week of the year – without paying tax. You may obtain a copy of the pay adjustment tables from your local tax office, or from your school or college finance department.

This is the first week of the tax year, so we start on week one. We look for the numbers in bold which correspond to tax codes. We need to look up Jonathan's tax code which as we saw earlier was 273L (see page 28). By looking for 273L in the bold lettering, we can easily see that in this first week of the tax year, Jonathan is allowed to earn £52.68 without paying tax. We can now enter this into the table.

Employee's name:					Tax code:				Year:		
Week no.	Pay on which NI to be paid	Employee's NI	Employer's NI	Total NI	Week no.	Pay in the week/ month	Total pay to date	Total free pay to date	Total taxable pay to date	Total tax due to date	Tax deducted or refunded
1					1	327.44	327.44				
2					2						
3					3						
4					4						
5					5						
6					6						
7					7						
8					8						
9					9						
10					10						

TABLE 3 *Tax-free pay*

So, if Jonathan earned £327.44 in week one, and has to pay tax on all of that except £52.68, that means he has to pay tax on £274.76. Put this information into the table.

Employee's name:					Tax code:				Year:		
Week no.	Pay on which NI to be paid	Employee's NI	Employer's NI	Total NI	Week no.	Pay in the week/ month	Total pay to date	Total free pay to date	Total taxable pay to date	Total tax due to date	Tax deducted or refunded
1					1	327.44	327.44	52.68	274.76		
2					2						
3					3						
4					4						
5					5						
6					6						
7					7						
8					8						
9					9						
10					10						

TABLE 4 *Taxable pay*

Recording financial information

Employee's name:					Tax code:				Year:		
Week no.	Pay on which NI to be paid	Employee's NI	Employer's NI	Total NI	Week no.	Pay in the week/ month	Total pay to date	Total free pay to date	Total taxable pay to date	Total tax due to date	Tax deducted or refunded
1					1	327.44	327.44	52.68	274.76	62.76	62.76
2					2						
3					3						
4					4						
5					5						
6					6						
7					7						
8					8						
9					9						
10					10						

TABLE 5 *Amount of tax paid*

Now we can find out exactly how much tax Jonathan will pay this week by looking in the second set of tax tables, known as 'taxable pay tables'. To obtain a copy of the taxable pay tables, contact your local tax office, or your school or college finance department. This does not have a different page for each week – all you have to do is look up the amount of taxable pay (in our case £274.76) in the bold numbers. If, as in our case, there are pounds and pence involved, you always round down to the nearest pound, which makes ours £274.00.

A little bit of addition is needed here as not every number is shown individually.

£200 = £48.00 payable tax
£74 = £17.76 payable tax
£274 therefore gives £65.76 payable tax

You would think that this was the amount of tax due, but there is one more adjustment to make. At the front of the taxable pay tables is a list of figures: one for each week of the year. This has to be deducted from the amount you just worked out because of adjustments by the government. For week one the amount is £3.00, therefore making Jonathan's tax bill for the week £62.76.

We can show this figure in the last column. However, as this is the first week, the same figure will also go in the penultimate column along, to show how much tax Jonathan has paid in the tax year as a whole.

In comparison to all of that, working out the amount of NI payable is easy. This requires one table named 'Not contracted out contributions'.

To obtain a copy of the tables for 'Not contracted out contributions', please refer to your local tax office, or your school or college finance department.

assignment

★ **EVIDENCE INDICATOR**

Summary which includes:

- a description of the main payroll documentation
- an explanation of the terms associated with payroll

★ **KEY SKILLS CONTRIBUTED TOWARDS**

IT
Communication

★ **TASKS**

1 Prepare an A5 booklet which could be used as a revision aid by GCSE Business pupils, which includes the following:

a) A description of the main payroll documentation consisting of: attendance records, national insurance tables, tax tables, payroll, payslips, standard national forms.

b) A glossary which explains the terms associated with payroll i.e.: wages, salaries, time rates, piece rates, bonus rates, annual rates, commission, deductions, gross pay, net pay.

Use pictures and diagrams to illustrate the points being made, as you see fit.

2 In a separate report, explain the importance of working safely and in line with good working practices, and explain the reason for using information technology to complete the above tasks.

★ **DEADLINE**

assignment

★ EVIDENCE INDICATOR

A summary which includes a description of the main payroll documentation and an explanation of the terms associated with payroll.

★ KEY SKILLS

Communication
IT

★ SCENARIO

You have been asked to take part in a discussion with the rest of your class on how the documentation which is used to record pay in businesses could be improved.

The discussion must be taped to provide evidence for your portfolio.

Arrange for a person who you know, but who is unfamiliar with the subject under discussion, to take part (such as a teacher who does not teach this unit).

★ TASKS

1. Make supporting notes on the subject, to prompt you in the discussion. These can then be used as evidence also.

2. When the discussion has concluded, write up an evaluation of how you believe it went, in the form of a memo to your teacher. Use the appropriate IT package to prepare this.

3. In small groups of three or four, discus with your classmates how you think the discussion above could have been improved. Again, you must tape this discussion.

★ DEADLINE

3

Recording and monitoring stock movements

Monitoring stock movements

To keep track of the stock held, businesses use procedures to control and monitor the movement of their stock. Some of these are detailed below.

CODES

For many products (especially those with long technical names whose details are stored on computer) it is much more efficient to use codes with which to reference them. One place where this can be seen is on a receipt from a supermarket. With hundreds of products to remember, a supermarket computer system would use up unnecessary space if it stored the full title of all the products. Therefore, to reduce the amount of storage space needed, codes are used.

BAR CODES

If you look on most items purchased in your weekly shopping – anything from nappies to chocolate – you will no doubt have noticed the sets of stripes which can be found on the labels. These are bar codes, and they are used for several different purposes. The most common one these days is to record the price of items at the checkouts of shops and supermarkets. This is completed with the help of EPOS terminals (Electronic Point of Sale). Whereas previously the checkout operator had to type in the price by hand now, when the bar code is scanned over a laser, the EPOS system recognises the individual make up of the bar code and puts the correct price into the calculation. The bar code stores other information as well, including the price and the name of the product and the manufacturer. In the event of the bar codes not scanning properly, the checkout operator enters a code which also contains the information.

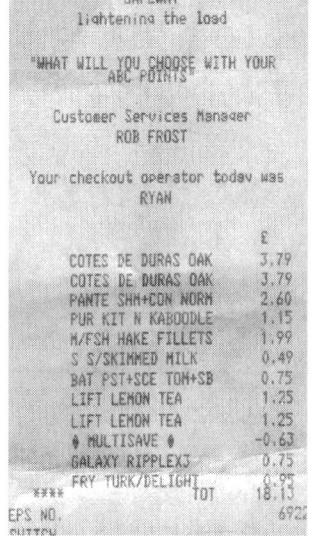

FIGURE 3.1 *Some examples of till receipts*

Recording and monitoring stock movements

FIGURE 3.2 *Scanning bar codes speeds up the checkout process*

> ### Key terms
>
> EPOS (Electronic Point of Sale) – Device commonly found in shops which retrieves information from a bar code to draw up the customer's bill.

FIGURE 3.3 *Some examples of bar codes*

AUTHORISATION

In many organisations there is no need for all employees to have access to the majority of stock. It therefore makes sense for authorised personnel only to handle the movement and distribution of stock. This could be accompanied by only authorised personnel holding keys to the stockroom, every item of stock being withdrawn having a docket signed by a manager to authorise its use, or employees having to sign for all stock withdrawn.

MANUAL STOCK MANAGEMENT VERSUS COMPUTER STOCK MANAGEMENT

Many organisations now record the movement of stock on a computer as opposed to just on the forms mentioned earlier. This has many advantages for both the business and its customers.

> **Key terms**
>
> Stock – Description given to the articles held by a business which are either for resale or to aid in the running of the business itself.

Advantages for the business ☺	Advantages for the customer ☺
Employees can find out how many – if any – of an item there are in stock	Customers can obtain up-to-the-minute information as to whether an item is in stock and, if not, how long it will take to be obtained
You do not have to physically look in the warehouse to see if a good is in stock	If enquiring over the phone about a product, the customer will not be kept waiting on the line longer than is absolutely necessary
Firms can take orders over the phone, confident that the product will be dispatched as soon as possible	If one branch of a business does not have the stock item, the customer can try another branch without delay

INVENTORY

An inventory (or stocktaking) takes place in all businesses at least once a year, and has several purposes:

- It forms the basis of the end of year stock valuation, which a company needs to draw up its year-end accounts
- It verifies that the systems a company has in place for the recording of stock receipts and issues are working
- It provides an exact picture of the amount of stock held by a company at any one time
- Although computer or manual records show how many of an item should be in stock, for various reasons (breakage, loss, age and shrinkage), the figures may not tally, and the company may think it owns more stock than it actually does
- It checks whether goods are being valued by the firm at the correct price.

This is either cost price (the price paid by the business for the goods) or the resale price (the price the business will get in return for the sale of the goods) – whichever is the lower. **Obviously cost price should be lower, or the business is in trouble!**

> **Key terms**
>
> **Sheet to shelf, shelf to sheet** – When checking the amount of stock held by a business, the person responsible (the auditor) will select a product at random and check to make sure that the amount of the product which is recorded by the business as being in stock actually exists. This is checking from sheet to shelf. A different product will then be picked and counted and the records of the business will be scrutinised, to check that the figures agree (shelf to sheet).

ISSUES SUMMARY AND STOCK BALANCES

As orders come in and out of the business it takes a while for the stock to physically move out of the business before it is sold. An issues summary is a way of recording the stock balance of any item – whether it has been removed from the premises or not.

Example

Fred works for Polly's Pine Palace, a furniture warehouse. At present, they have a stock balance of 20 pine beds. On Monday, Fred receives an order to deliver 12 of the beds the following week. This would leave a balance of eight beds. He makes a note of this in the issues summary. This means that in reality, Polly's Pine Palace can now only sell a maximum of eight pine beds before re-ordering. On Wednesday, Fred receives another order for 10 beds to be delivered on the same day as the first order. He knows he has 20 beds in the warehouse *but* by looking in the issues summary, he sees that 12 of them are spoken for, and that he must obtain more stock before he can fulfil the second order.

RE-ORDER LEVELS

When companies re-order their stock, they do not simply pick a figure out of the air and hope for the best. They order an amount which is commensurate with their predicted future needs and what they can afford. Let's go back to Fred at Polly's Pine Palace.

Fred could have avoided the problem by ensuring that the companies stock re-order

FIGURE 3.4 *Efficient stock-checking reduces delays in meeting orders.*

levels are always sufficient to cover most eventualities. It is not expected that Fred should predict an order for 100 beds if the largest order ever received was for 30. However, to run efficiently, there should always be enough stock to cover everyday orders. This means that when the stock level falls below a certain pre-defined figure (X), an order is automatically sent out to bring the stock up to another pre-defined level (Y). This way, management – and Fred – know that as far as possible the company always has between X and Y amount of stock available at any one time.

UNITS

Some products are supplied in single units (i.e. you buy one of them at a time) such as a car or a stereo. However, most everyday items can also be bought in twos, threes or more (e.g. in bulk) such as baked beans, biros and burgers! In this case, it is essential that the units of stock are clearly marked. For instance, if you were to work in a warehouse and you were asked to put three biros on a lorry, you would be incorrect if you actually put three biros in. As the units that warehouses work in are in bulk, you should therefore have put in three boxes of biros instead!

When ordering goods, order forms have a column for units, so that it is absolutely clear how many of an item are required. This avoids mistakes and confusion at a later stage, as in the example above.

ORDERS

As seen in the example where Fred had to order some more beds before they could be sold to the customer, companies have to order goods from other companies before they can sell them on, either to other companies or customers. This is called the chain of distribution: in other words, how the goods get from the manufacturer to the customer. We have already looked at order forms and their contents in chapter one.

RECEIPTS

When a good that has been ordered arrives at the organisation which placed the order, it is termed a receipt. This does not refer to the type of receipt you get at a supermarket checkout as seen earlier, but to the fact that the goods have been received. Different organisations process receipts in a variety of different ways, however, it is prudent to check that the goods which are being delivered are those that were ordered, that the correct quantity has been delivered and that no damages have occurred in transit (see returns day book on page 12).

ISSUES

When a company has completed the two steps above, it can then issue the goods it has ordered to its customers. These goods may leave the firm in the same state as they came in, or, if the company manufactures goods, they may leave as part of a different product. Whichever they are, they are still issues.

assignment

★ **EVIDENCE INDICATOR**

Presentation on the recording and monitoring of stock movements.

★ **KEY SKILLS**

IT
Communication
Application of Number

★ **SCENARIO**

You work in the warehouse of a large distribution company dealing with the everyday movement of stock and the paperwork that accompanies it. You have a new boss starting in three week's time who has very little idea of stock control and what it entails. Your existing boss has asked you to prepare a brief on the following points, to get the new boss familiarised as quickly as possible.

★ **TASKS**

1 Explain the terms commonly associated with recording stock movements.

2 Work through the scenario above using the appropriate records and present the answer with accompanying notes where applicable.

3 Explain the various security checks used for controlling the movement of stock.

4 For the scenario in task 2, explain the following:
 - An issues summary
 - Stock balances
 - Re-order levels.

★ **DEADLINE**

assignment

EVIDENCE INDICATOR

A presentation on the recording and monitoring of stock movements.

SCENARIO

Along with two or three other students, you are to give a presentation (which may be aided by suitable visual aids) which covers the following points:

- An explanation of the terms associated with recording stock movement
- An explanation of security checks for recording stock movement.

TASKS

1 With the rest of your group, discus how you intend to divide up the workload. Get your teacher to observe this and write a verbal evidence sheet or tape the discussions for evidence in your portfolio.

2 Prepare the visual aids which will accompany your part of the presentation. These can be either static (OHPs, posters) or moving (video, Power Point presentation etc).

3 Arrange a practice run-through of your presentation to iron out any bugs.

4 When delivering your presentation, ensure that it is tape recorded or videoed.

★ **DEADLINE**

4
Monitoring transactions against a given budget

Just as financial planning is an important part of the life of any business organisation, so budgeting is also a part of the planning process. A good business person knows that it is vital to plan ahead. If they do not, any unexpected occurrences (large bills, repairs etc.) may cause problems.

> ### Key terms
> A budget is a detailed plan for a period of time in the future. It can be a plan for a short period of time or a long period of time, for a specific project or for a whole company.

Purposes of budget setting

MONITORING AGAINST TARGETS (INCOME AND EXPENDITURE)

Any successful business will constantly set and review targets relating to its performance in many areas. This could be in the training of staff, in gaining the Investors in People (IIP) award, in installing a new computer system or in organising a social function. The targets could be performance-related, but they will also include a monetary value. Firms monitor their income and expenditure according to the targets they have to achieve. This way, if either the income or expenditure are not as predicted, then further investigation can take place. This will undoubtedly help in the achievement of the aforementioned targets.

> ### Key terms
> IIP (Investors in People) – This is an award given to companies in recognition of their approach to the training and development of their employees.

PLANNING THE USE OF RESOURCES

No organisation has unlimited resources – it is therefore vital that any resources which are available to a company are used in the right place, at the right time, for the right purpose. Planning how these resources are used is another form of budgeting and, again, part of the setting and reviewing of targets for any organisation. The more a firm plans the use of its resources, and the more thought goes into their use within the organisation, the higher the chances are that the organisation will reach its targets.

PERSONAL BUDGET

At some times in your life you may find yourself with enough money to buy extra things such as holidays or a car, and at others you may find you hardly have enough money for your bus fare! It helps if you can draw up a personal budget to make sure that you have enough money available to cover your basic outgoings for as long as possible – and still be able to afford luxuries at other times too.

When drawing up a personal budget you have to look at two areas:

- Your *income* – money that you receive

FIGURE 4.1 *Budgeting is a vital part of planning ahead*

- Your **expenditure** – money that you spend.

INCOME

When making a list of your different sources of income, it will (to some extent) depend upon what time of year it is – just like in a lot of businesses. For instance, you may have a part-time job which provides you with a steady weekly, or fortnightly or even monthly income. However, it is also a safe bet that you may have other, less frequent, sources of income such as pocket money from parents or grandparents, income from celebrations such as birthdays or Christmas, and money from odd jobs (car washing etc.). There are many sources of income and these will no doubt vary from individual to individual – think about where the money comes from that you receive, and try to estimate how much you receive from each source over a given period of time. The example on page 47 is over a period of four months.

The planning and forecasting of income

Companies also have to predict how much money is going to enter the business over a period of time. This could be through the following sources:

★ Sale of goods/services
★ Returns on investments
★ Loans
★ Sale of assets
★ Grants

Recording financial information

FIGURE 4.2 *A part-time job can help you understand budgeting*

★ Investment from other sources.

If the company does not have an idea as to how much income it will receive, then it cannot adequately plan for its future. It needs to know how much it can spend, and whether it will have any spare cash to invest in new equipment and machinery etc.

EXPENDITURE

I doubt if there are any two people in the country who spend exactly the same amount of money on identical items every week. Therefore, a personal budget is an individual thing and, although it is good to compare your budget with other people to see how they have laid their's out, your income and expenditure will be unique to you. However, you may be able to get some tips on how to reduce your expenditure by comparing how much you spend on items such as travel.

The control and monitoring of expenditure

Just as a company needs to plan and forecast its income, it must also control and monitor its expenditure to ensure that the careful planning that has gone into the rest of the business is not undone by some careless spending. This can be done in several ways. In most businesses it is done by setting budgets either for projects, departments or managers. It is then the responsibility of the head of a project or department to make sure that, if possible, they spend only what has been allocated to them in the budget. Depending on the size of the company and the purpose of the budget, the amounts can vary from a few hundred pounds to millions.

One problem which occurs with budgets is when they are under-used. It is common practice for a department to have its budget reduced in the following year if the whole budget has not been used up in the preceding year. This is a short-sighted way to look at budgets. It often means that, at the end of a company's financial year, managers and budget holders spend money quickly, often on items which may not be really

	Budget				
	September	October	November	December	Total
In					
Balance b/f (bring forward)	500	422	857	992	
Wages	1000	1000	1000	1000	4000
Other	0	300	0	0	300
Total in	1500	1722	1857	1992	
Out					
Mortgage	200	200	200	200	800
Insurance 1	60	60	60	60	240
Insurance 2	25	25	25	25	100
Loan	225	225	225	225	1140
Shopping	80	80	80	80	320
Gas	25	25	25	25	100
Electric	63	0	0	70	133
Water	40	40	40	40	160
Postage	10	10	10	10	40
Council tax	40	40	40	40	160
Credit card 1	40	40	40	40	160
Credit card 2	30	30	30	30	120
Student loan	15	15	15	15	60
Hire purchase	60	60	60	60	240
Telephone	150	0	0	100	250
Transport	15	15	15	15	60
Total out	1078	865	865	1035	
Balance c/f (carried forward)	422	857	992	957	

FIGURE 4.3 *An example of a personal budget*

necessary just so that the budget is not reduced in the following year. The most prevalent example of this is in local government departments, where huge sums are spent before the end of the financial year – on all sorts of items.

> ### Key terms
>
> Local government – The organisation responsible for carrying out the wishes of Parliament at a local level, such as in the provision of education and health services.

FIGURE 4.4 *A successful event needs careful planning*

assignment

★ **EVIDENCE INDICATOR**

Record of monitoring of transactions against a given budget.

★ **KEY SKILLS CONTRIBUTED TOWARDS**

IT
Communication
Application of Number

★ **SCENARIO**

You have been asked to organise an evening function where certificates will be awarded to the students who have completed their GNVQ in the last academic year (see Figure 4.4).

You have been allocated a budget of £500 with which to provide the following:

- Decorations for the room in which the function is to take place
- Buffet for 50 people
- Soft drinks for 50 people
- Five gift tokens of £15 in value – as prizes
- Table decorations for ten tables (five people per table)
- One trophy for the 'Student of the Year' award.

TASKS

1 As an introduction to the assignment, provide an explanation of the purposes of budget setting.

2 Collect prices from the appropriate sources for the items above.

Note: Collect more than one price for each, to ensure the best value is obtained.

3 Prepare a record of your planned expenditure for the items. Are you within budget?

4 Prepare a plan of the layout of the venue for the function and label appropriately.

★ **SCENARIO CONTINUED:**

You are now informed that there will be ten additional guests at the function.

5 Amend your record of expenditure as appropriate. Are you still within budget?

6 As a conclusion, identify what variations could have occurred within your budget, and explain how your final purchase decisions make sense in respect of the problem being tackled.

7 If you used IT to prepare this assignment, describe the software facilities used to meet the requirements of the task.

★ **DEADLINE**

Multiple-choice questions

Multi-choice questions

The following questions will assess the knowledge you have gained from this book and will help you to find out whether you have fully understood a topic.

1 Which of the documents below is NOT a legal requirement for a company to produce?
   a) VAT return
   b) Payslip
   c) Income tax return
   d) Returns day book

2 Which of the documents below monitors the income **and** expenditure within a business?
   a) Purchase ledger
   b) Cash book
   c) Sales day book
   d) Returns day book

3 What is the purpose of the sales day book?
   a) To plan how many items the firm needs to sell in the coming year
   b) To record the amount of sales made on a given day
   c) To record the level of sales of a company's competitors
   d) To give the accounts clerk something to do in the morning

4 VAT is calculated at what percentage on most goods in the UK?
   a) 20 per cent
   b) 15.5 per cent
   c) 10 per cent
   d) 17.5 per cent

5 Which of the following is NOT recorded on an order form?
   a) The address of the goods are to be delivered to
   b) The date the order was placed
   c) The amount of goods found to be faulty in the order
   d) The price for each unit of the goods required

6 Which one of the following is NOT a valid way of recording the number of hours worked by an employee?
   a) A 100-minute hour clock card
   b) A timesheet
   c) A scrap of paper handed into the wages office on Friday
   d) A 60-minute hour clock card

7 National insurance is used by the government to pay for which of the following?
   a) Pension
   b) Education
   c) Road maintenance
   d) The Civil List

8 Both employer and employee contribute to the national insurance paid to the government.
   a) True
   b) False

9 Income tax is paid by everybody who works.
   a) True
   b) False

10 What is the name of the document on which the names of a firm's employees are recorded?
   a) Payslip
   b) Payroll
   c) Pay off
   d) Sick pay

11 Which of the following pieces of information does not have to be included in an employee's payslip?
   a) Gross pay
   b) Net pay
   c) Address of employee
   d) National insurance contributions

12 Which of the following is not a common Standard National Form?
   a) P45
   b) P60

c) P46
   d) P101

13 Which of the following jobs is most likely to be paid a wage?
   a) Fast-food restaurant worker
   b) Teacher
   c) Nurse
   d) Doctor

14 PRP stands for which of the following?
   a) Pay Really Poor
   b) Performance Related Pay
   c) Purchase Rope Products
   d) Please Read Promptly

15 Which of the following jobs is most likely to be paid by commission?
   a) Double-glazing salesperson
   b) Dentist
   c) An electrician
   d) Teacher

16 The initials 'p.a.' related to a salary, stand for which of the following?
   a) Pay award
   b) Personal allowance
   c) Paid a lot
   d) Per annum

17 Gross pay is your pay after deductions.
   a) True
   b) False

18 On which set of tax tables do we find out how much tax an individual will pay?
   a) Taxable Pay tables
   b) Pay Adjustment tables
   c) Not Contracted out contributions
   d) Table A

19 When storing long product names on the computer, which of the following saves time and memory?
   a) Typing in half the name of the product
   b) Using codes to identify products
   c) Learning to type faster
   d) Buying a more powerful computer

20 EPOS stands for which of the following?
   a) Electronic Pint of Soup
   b) Electrically Posted Order System
   c) Electronic Point of Sale
   d) Easy Peasy Order System

21 The cost price of a good should be lower than its resale price.
   a) True
   b) False

22 What is the name of the procedure where an auditor will check both the amount of stock in the stockroom, and the amount recorded in the stock records?
   a) Check stock – check book
   b) Stock room – stock record
   c) Sheet to shelf – shelf to sheet
   d) Double-check stock check

23 Everybody has the same items in their personal budget.
   a) True
   b) False

24 A budget is prepared to plan for a period of time in the future.
   a) True
   b) False

25 Which of the following is not a source of income for an organisation?
   a) Sale of goods/services
   b) Grants
   c) Buying a new computer
   d) Loans

26 Which of the following is not a type of expenditure for an organisation?
   a) Wages

    b) Insurance
    c) National insurance
    d) Sale of assets

27 Which of the following can be both a source of income and expenditure to an organisation?
    a) Bank interest
    b) National insurance
    c) Income tax
    d) Wages

28 Who announces changes to the basic rate of income tax?
    a) The Prime Minister
    b) The Chancellor of the Exchequer
    c) The Foreign Minister
    d) Your local borough council

29 What is the basic rate of income tax?
    a) 25 per cent
    b) 24 per cent
    c) 23 per cent
    d) 22 per cent

30 If you store information about individuals on a computer, you have to comply with the Data Protection Act of 1984.
    a) True
    b) False

See page 58 for the answers.

Glossary

Amplification Clarifies key terms used in the element, sometimes with examples.

Assets Items owned by a company which can range in size and function.

At source Term which defines how deductions are taken away from an individual's pay, before it is received.

Attendance records Record of how many hours an employee has worked within a certain time frame. Can be recorded on a clock card or timesheet.

Auditor A person who checks a company is conducting their financial affairs properly.

Bar code Series of lines and stripes commonly found on packages which contain information about the manufacturer and price etc.

Blue-collar workers Those employed in manual, unskilled or semi-skilled occupations and usually paid a wage.

Bonus rates An extra sum added to an employee's wage or salary as an extra reward.

Budget A specified amount of money or resources allocated to a project, department or individual.

Cash book Used to keep a record of a company's income and expenditure.

Clock cards One form of attendance record. A card is placed into a machine and the time recorded on the card.

Commission A percentage added to a person's wage or salary (usually sales people) commensurate with the volume of sales gained.

Database Software package on which a large amount of data can be stored.

Deductions Money which is taken out of an individual's gross pay such as income tax and national insurance.

Discounts A percentage or amount deducted from the total amount outstanding on a purchase, usually for bulk buying or for prompt payment.

Electronic Point of Sale (EPOS) Device commonly found in shops which retrieves

Glossary

information from a bar code to draw up the customer's bill.

Element Lays out the skills, knowledge and understanding required in detail and indicates how students should present the evidence.

Employees Individuals who provide their labour in return for payment.

Expenditure Money which is used by an individual or an organisation to purchase goods or services.

Grant A source of income for businesses which does not have to be repaid. Can be awarded by the government.

Gross pay The pay an individual has earned before any deductions are taken off.

Guidance Provides advice for teachers on delivery and indicates links between elements.

Halo effect Term used to describe how people think highly of an individual in one area of life, when they only really know their performance in other areas.

Income Money which is received by either an individual or an organisation.

Income tax A percentage of an individual's wage or salary which pays for government spending.

Information Technology The use of computer-aided equipment to complete tasks more efficiently.

Invoice Document sent from a supplier to a customer, detailing goods supplied.

Issue summary An up-to-the-minute account of the amount of stock which is available for use in an organisation.

Loan Source of income for businesses and individuals which has to be repaid, normally with interest added.

Manager Person responsible for deploying an organisation's resources and making policy decisions.

National insurance A percentage of an individual's wage or salary, and a contribution from his/her employer, which provides money for government-provided services.

Net pay The pay an individual actually receives, after deductions.

Order How an individual or organisation buys goods from another individual or organisation – usually placed on an order form.

Overtime An increase in the amount a person is paid per hour, when working over the contracted hours for a time period.

Payslip Source of information about pay and deductions.

Payroll Record of all the employees paid by an organisation.

Pension Amount of money received after a person has retired or finished work. A state pension (provided by the government) is paid after the age of 65.

Performance related pay (PRP) An extra sum added to an employee's salary as a reward for completing their job successfully.

Piece rates A pay system where an employee is paid according to the number of units of a good manufactured.

Purchase day book Used to record all purchases made in an organisation.

Re-order levels The minimum and maximum amount of stock a company works with to ensure best use is made of the company's resources.

Returns day book A record of any items

which have been returned to an organisation.

Salary   Pay which is received by white-collar workers and is paid monthly, varying little between pay-days.

Sales day book   A record of all the money which is owed to an organisation. Invoices are recorded in this.

Shrinkage   Term used to describe the loss of stock through theft.

Standard National Forms   A set of forms issued by the government to help collect information about employees.

Stocktaking   Usually an annual event for all businesses. The information collected is used to construct the annual accounts.

Supplier   Person from whom goods or services are bought.

Tax code   Information which tells individuals and their employers how much money can be earned during the tax year, without paying tax.

Tax year   The financial year as used by the government and businesses which runs from 6 April to 5 April.

Time rates   The pay awarded per hour – mostly in manual jobs.

Value Added Tax (VAT)   A percentage added to the price of goods sold by businesses, which is collected by HM Customs and Excise.

Wages   Pay which is (usually) received by blue-collar workers. Can be awarded hourly and paid weekly. Can vary each pay-day.

References

Business and Finance for BTEC First and GNVQ, 1st edn.
Gill Clarke and Roger Lewis (1992)
Published by Stanley Thornes (Publishes) Ltd, Old Station Drive, Leckhampton, Cheltenham, GL53 0DN
Pages 135, 145, 207–211.

Business Intermediate GNVQ Mandatory and Core Skills Units Specifications, 1st edn. (1995)
Published and copyright held by BTEC at Central House, Upper Woburn Place, London WC1H 0HH
Pages 8–9.

Business Intermediate GNVQ Optional Units Specifications, 1st edn. (1995)
Published and copyright held by BTEC at Central House, Upper Woburn Place, London, WC1H 0HH
Pages 14–18.

Financial Planning and Monitoring. 1st edn.
Karl Smith (1995)
Published and copyright held by Pitman Publishing, 128 Long Acre, London, WC2E 9AN
Pages 21–23.

Answers to multiple-choice questions

1 d)	**7** a)	**13** a)	**19** b)	**25** c)
2 b)	**8** a)	**14** b)	**20** c)	**26** d)
3 b)	**9** b)	**15** a)	**21** a)	**27** a)
4 d)	**10** b)	**16** d)	**22** c)	**28** b)
5 c)	**11** c)	**17** b)	**23** b)	**29** c)
6 c)	**12** d)	**18** a)	**24** a)	**30** a)

Index

accounting records
  cash books 8, 9
  invoices 8, 12, 14
  order forms 12, 13
  purchase day books 8, 10
  returns day books 11–12
  sales day books 10–11
attendance records 18–19
auditors 38

bar codes 36–7
bonuses 24, 26
budgets 44, 46, 48

cash books 8, 9
chain of distribution 40
clock cards 18–19, 28
codes
  stock 36
  tax 30
commission 26
computers
  record keeping 15
  stock management 38

discounts 11

emergency tax 24
EPOS (Electronic Point of Sale) terminals 36–7
expenditure 46

forecasting 45–6

gross pay 27, 29

income 45–6
income tax 20
information technology (IT) 15
inventories 38
Investors in People (IIP) award 44
invoices 8, 12, 14
issues summary 39

local government 48

monitoring performance 8, 44

National Insurance (NI) 19–20, 32
net pay 27

order forms 12, 13
overtime 26

P45 23–4
pay adjustment tables 30
payrolls 20–2
payslips 22–3
performance monitoring 8, 44
performance-related pay (PRP) 24
personal budgets 44–5, 47
piece rates 26–7
planning 44, 45–6
purchase day books 8, 10

re-order levels 39–40
receipts 40

resources 44
returns day books 11–12

salaries 24, 25, 27
sales day books 10–11
standard national forms (SNF) 23–4
statutory accounting requirements 7
stock movement
  authorisation 37
  bar codes 36–7
  computerised 38
  inventories (stocktaking) 38
  issues summary 39
  re-order levels 39–40
  receipts 40
  stock codes 36
stockrooms 37
stocktaking 38
suppliers 10

targets 8, 44
tax
  codes 30
  emergency tax 24
  income tax 20
  pay adjustment tables 30
  standard national forms (SNF) 23–4
  tax forms 29
  tax tables 29, 30
  taxable pay tables 31–2
  VAT (Value Added Tax) 7, 8, 10
tax-free pay 31
till receipts 36
timesheets 19

units of stock 40

VAT (Value Added Tax) 7, 8, 10

wages 24, 25